Salamanders

For Kids

Amazing Animal Books

for Young Readers

By Zahra Jazeel and John Davidson

Mendon Cottage Books

JD-Biz Corp Publishing

Read More Amazing Animal Books

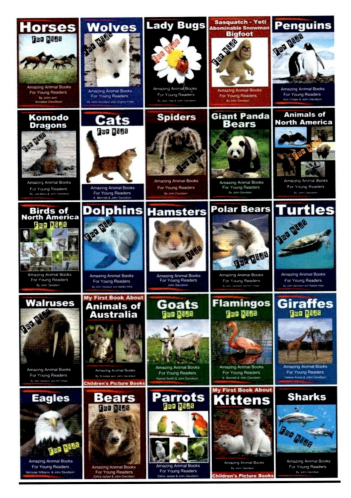

Purchase at Amazon.com

Table of Contents

Introduction

Most of you can name at least 2 or 3 different breeds of dogs or even cats when asked. They are common animals that we encounter almost every day. But will you be able to answer if asked to name at least one species of salamander? Some may even wonder whether there are many types in this creature after this question is posed to them. But luckily you don't have to wrack your brain to search for answers as we provide you with all the facts that you need to know about salamanders in this fun book! Learn some fascinating facts about a unique, and a not-so-common animal.

Come on and join us as we try to explore about salamanders, their features, senses, feeding habits, defensive mechanisms, species and many more!

About Salamanders

Salamanders have an appearance of a lizard with blunt snouts, slender bodies and short limbs that are situated at right angles to the body. Tail is present both in the larva as well as adults. Salamanders do not have more than 5 toes on their hind legs and 4 toes on their front legs, though some appear to lack hind legs and some have lesser number of digits. The skin that they possess is unique and permeable. This allows them to live near cool, damp places with water though some species completely prefer to live their life in water or on land. In legends and literature, salamanders were portrayed as creatures that cannot be harmed by fire. Clothes made of their skin are thought to be incombustible. That is, it does not catch fire.

Another very interesting thing about salamanders is their ability to regenerate or regrow lost limps or other parts if damaged. Even today, several researches are carried out to investigate its potential usage for human medicine. Some species of salamanders possess a deadly poison known as tetrodotoxin on their skin. These salamanders move slowly and warn about their toxicity by displaying bright colored skin on the surface.

External Features

General physical features of an adult salamander are four limbs, cylindrical trunk and a long tail. This is similar to the general form of a small lizard. Some species adapted to a lifestyle in water have less or no hind limbs making them appear like an eel. In many species, both the front and the hind limbs are equal in length project sideways. Short digits are present on their broad feet. Salamanders do not possess claws. The shape of their feet varies depending on their habitat. For example, webbed feet with a plate like appearance is found on tree climbing salamanders whereas short blunt toes on large feet is found on rock dwellers.

Laterally flattened tails are possessed by aquatic salamanders and larvae. The tail serves as a self-defense weapon against predators. It can also store lipids and proteins. The skin of a salamander is thin and delicate. It is well equipped with glands. These glands release mucus. Mucus helps to keep the skin wet and moist. Water can enter and leave through the skin. Hence it is permeable to water. The skin acts as a respiratory membrane. That means it aids salamanders to breathe through skin.

Snakes shed their skin. Similarly, salamanders also shed their skin. After shedding, they eat their sloughed skin.

Senses

The sense of smell in salamanders plays a major role in identifying predators and territorial maintenance. But their vision is the primary sense that is used when selecting the prey and feeding. In order to respond to the changes in the environment, salamanders possess 2 types of sensory areas. The cavity in the nasal area is lined by a group of cells known as olfactory epithelium that helps in picking up odours both in air and water. Another organ adjoined to this organ helps in detecting sense such as taste.

Most salamanders use their eyes primarily for night vision. Some species permanently adapted for a life in water have eyes that are small in size. The Georgia blind salamander, a type of cave dweller has no eyes and in some, they are covered by a layer of skin. The fire salamander, a type of salamander totally adapted for a life on land have lens that are flat and could focus over a vast distance.

The fish has an organ that could detect pressure changes in water. Similarly, adults and larvae of some highly aquatic species have developed a similar organ to identify changes in water pressure. Though salamanders are considered to have no voice, some species are known to make popping and quiet ticking sounds. Few other species can squeak, hiss and click too.

Diet

Salamanders are opportunistic feeders. Their diet is not restricted to certain foods in particular. Hence they prey on any organism that is of reasonable size. The Japanese giant salamander, a large species, is known to have consumed aquatic insects, fish, amphibians, crabs and even small mammals. The dusky salamander, a small species of salamanders found to live in Appalachian Mountains consume flies, beetles and earthworms. Sometimes cannibalism is reported to have taken place mainly when the resources go short. Cannibalism is the act of feeding on the same species.

Many salamander species have teeth on both upper and lower jaws. They are small. The teeth of an adult salamander are adapted to grasp its prey readily. Even the larval from of salamanders possess teeth. They are small and look pointed like cones. It is very interesting to note that the teeth of salamanders get resorbed, that is break into its former constituents and then gets replaced at certain intervals throughout its life.

Frogs have a sticky tongue which they use to flick and catch small preys. Similarly, a salamander that is well adapted to the life on land flicks its sticky tongue to catch its prey. The tongue is sticky due to the mucus secretions from glands present on its mouth.

Defense Mechanisms

Salamanders are vulnerable to predators at first glance due to their small, soft bodies with thin skins accompanied by a slow movement. However, they have a line of self-defensive tactics up their sleeves. Their skin is dump due to the mucus coating. This makes it quite slippery for the predators to grasp and hold it still. The slimy coat could give off a bad taste or could be toxic. Some salamanders when attacked by a predator will try to position themselves so as to make their major poison glands to be faced by the enemy. Most often, they are present on their tails which could be wagged or arched at any position. The strategy of losing its tail could be a valuable sacrifice if the salamander is spared with its life and the predator learns its lesson to not approach a salamander of that type.

It was observed that when a tiger salamander's skin secretions were fed to rats, the rats avoided it when it was presented to them the second time. The fire salamander has the ability to squirt toxic fluid from its spine by angling its body correctly. This could be sprayed up to a distance of 80cm. Some salamanders use their body color to display their toxicity. Orange, red and yellow are the usual colors often accompanied with black for better contrast.

Myths and Legends

Many legends have been wound around salamanders for several centuries. Many are related to the element, fire. The first evidence for this appeared in ancient Greece. Salamanders were known to dwell in rotting logs. Hence when the logs are placed on fire, they try to escape possibly leading to the myth that they are made of flames. Prester John, a mythical ruler was known to have had a robe made of salamander hair. A suit made of 1000 salamander skins was owned by the emperor of India. Even Pope Alexander III possessed a tunic that he valued so dearly. Furthermore, salamanders were believed to be very toxic so much so that if it was twined around a tree, it could possibly poison the fruits and kill anyone who eats them.   If it was dropped into a well, the whole well would be poisoned and the people who drink from it could also get killed.

In Japan, the Japanese giant salamander had been a subject for artworks and legends. 'Kappa' is a well-known mythological creature from japan. The salamander might have inspired the creation of 'kappa'. In Matilda, a children's' book written by Roald Dahl, a newt is starred as a key player in the first chapter.

Tiger salamander

The Tiger salamander is found living across North America in wetland habitats. Have you ever wondered why its called the 'Tiger' salamander? They are called Tiger salamanders because of the dark colored markings present on their skin which resembles a tiger. They have a long tail and sturdy legs. There is one special ability worth mentioning. If their limbs get damaged or lost due to some reason, they will regrow automatically. Though this salamander is called the tiger salamander, the proper common name is 'eastern tiger salamander'. The typical length of a Tiger salamander is 15-20cm. But this can be grown to a maximum of 36 cm. Generally, the adults are green, black or grey with dark markings. They have thick necks and short snouts. The eyes are large but lidded.

They mainly consume worms and small insects. However, the adults also prey on baby mice and small frogs. Tiger salamanders live partly on land and water. Seeing an adult salamander in the open is a rare sight as they usually live in burrows one or two feet above the surface. Tiger salamanders are great swimmers. Common predators of them are coatis, river turtles, raccoons large reptiles and birds.

Flatwoods salamander

From Wikimedia Commons

Flatwoods salamanders are medium in size. They are endemic to Atlantic coastal plains and lower Gulf regions. Historically known longleaf pine-wiregrass flatwoods or savannahs are their habitats. In recent years, their habitats have declined lesser than 20% of its original area. Flatwoods salamanders that are living now are small and highly vulnerable to habitat loss and fragmentation. In this case, fragmentation refers to scattering of this species.

The usual color of a Flatwoods salamander ranges from chocolate black to normal black with irregular specks and fine light grey lines creating a cross banded pattern on its back . Adult salamanders prefer to live underground most of their years as they are adapted to a terrestrial lifestyle. In other words, an earthly life. These salamanders were split into 2 species according to a new research. They are the Reticulated Flatwoods salamander and the Frosted Flatwoods salamander. Under the endangered Species Act of 1999, the Flatwoods salamanders were listed as a threated species. This species is among the hardest to locate out of all the other member species because they are declining. Scattered populations were found in restricted habitats of Georgia, South Carolina and Florida. But they were not seen in Alabama since the beginning of 1970.

Northwestern salamander

Northwestern salamanders are found living in North America, particularly inhabiting the North West pacific coast. Adults living in terrestrial environments inhabit grasslands or mesophytic forests. Mesophytes are terrestrial plants that are not adapted to either wet or dry environments. Though North western salamanders are not easy to be found, they appear to be in good state. They have the ability to inhabit many forested habitats while avoiding dangerous predators.

These salamanders are quite large growing to a maximum length of 24cm. The usual body color is dark brown though some individuals appear to be black or grey. Sometimes light flecks could be seen on their backs. Both young and adult salamanders have big dark bulging eyes. The head of an adult is broad. The tail is vertically flat and their hind legs are large, perfectly suited for burrowing or swimming. Salamanders adapted for a terrestrial lifestyle consume small invertebrates. Invertebrate is an animal without a backbone. However, the hatchlings feed on small crustaceans. Crustaceans are animals with segmented soft bodies and a hard outer shell. Some examples for aquatic crustaceans are shrimps, crabs and lobsters. As the hatchlings grow, they tend to feed on larger preys such as worms, fairy shrimps, insect larvae, tadpoles and snails.

Jefferson salamander

From USDA Public Domain

Jefferson salamander is native to some parts in Canada, America and Quebec. How did a salamander get the name of Jefferson? Actually, the salamanders were named after a Pennsylvanian College known as the Jefferson College. These types of salamanders are usually black, brown or dark grey in color. However, a lighter shade is present on the front part of their body. In some individuals, blue or silver specks are seen on the sides.

Jefferson salamanders are slender and can grow from 11 to 18cm. They have long distinct toes and a nose that is wide. These salamanders burrow. That is, they dig a hole or a tunnel underground in order to live. They are nocturnal creatures which means they are active during night time. Both larval and adult forms are carnivores consuming only animal matter. The larvae feed on aquatic invertebrates while adults feed on many small invertebrates. Sometimes cannibalism is reported when food becomes insufficient.

Adult Jefferson salamanders are known to hide underneath logs, stones or leaves in wet conditions. But they are not seen in forests which are home to conifers, trees that bear needle like leaves with cones. This could be due to the prickly nature of these trees which could possibly injure their delicate skins.

Long- toed salamander

Long-toedSalamander <u>Thompsma</u> From Wikimedia Commons

The body of a long toed salamander is mottled with brown, black or yellow colours. They are easily distinguished by their long fourth toe on their hind limbs. Adults reach up to a length between 4.1 and 8.9cm. Long toed salamanders primarily inhabit the Pacific Northwest. They live in a wide variety of environments including red fir forest, coniferous forests, temperate rainforests, alpine meadows and sagebrush plains. Hibernation is a process in which on organism passes the winter in an inactive state either by resting or sleeping. Long toed salamanders hibernate on winter surviving on stored energy reserves in its skin and tail. However, some adults from lowland areas do not hibernate and stay active throughout the winter. The IUCN (International Union for Conservation of Nature) has enlisted the Long toed salamander under the 'least Concern' category despite the lingering threats to their habitat.

If you wish to see an adult, try looking for them in small mammal burrows or under rocks and woody debris. But if you want to see them on the breeding season of spring, then you may have to change course and head onto shallow shorelines of lakes, ponds, rivers and streams. Long toed salamander is the second most abundant salamander in North America right after the Tiger salamander.

Cave salamander

The term 'cave salamander' is commonly referred to several salamander species that inhibit caves exclusively or primarily. It is really interesting note that some of these creatures have developed certain adaptations to suit this lifestyle. Having a not- so- highly developed eyes with poor vision is one such adaptation. Due to this reason, these salamanders are also called the 'blind salamanders'. Pigments are responsible in providing color to skin. However, these animals lack pigments on their skin. Hence they are either pinkish or pale yellow in color due to the presence of blood capillaries that are visible due to the translucency of their skin. Due to this bizarre appearance that resembled a small human, people used to call them as 'human fish'.

The total length of a cave salamander ranges between 23 to 25cm. They can even grow up to 30cm or more than that in rare instances. When it comes to size, males are slightly smaller than the females. Four limbs of a cave salamander are short and weak. The head has an elongated shape with a snout that is round. The tail is flat and noticeably shorter than the trunk section.

Red Hills salamander

From USGS Public Domain Wikimedia Commons

Red Hills salamanders are adapted to live a terrestrial lifestyle. They are quite large in size capable of growing up to 10 inches in length. The body could be grey or brownish in color with no markings. They possess a long tail, prominent eyes and a slender body which is easily distinguishable. However there are 2 distinct features present in this type of salamanders. First is the presence of a narrow groove that lies in between the nostril and the upper lip. Second is the presence of mental glands. Though this sounds to appear in connection with the head or the brain, it is not so. In fact, they are specialized mucus glands capable of releasing pheromones. Pheromones are chemicals that can influence other member's behavior. Sometimes, these glands are visible as raised bumps in males just below their lower lip.

The Red Hill salamander is the official amphibian for the state of Alabama. They prefer living in burrows which are present in the slopes of cool, damp ravines that are shaded by hardwood trees. This species is a threatened species due to habitat loss, restricted range and low birth rate. Did you know that these creatures are capable of spending about 12 hours at the mouth of its burrow so that it could feed on some forest floor insects?

Northern zigzag salamander

Plethodon dorsalis by berichard From Wikimedia Commons

Northern zigzag salamanders are small in size growing up to a length between 2.5 to 3.5 inches. The zigzag salamanders were recently spilt into 2 as Northern zigzag salamanders and the Southern zigzag salamanders. Both look identical. The former has a body with a red or an orange zigzag pattern which runs down from the neck to the base of its tail. Some individuals have a brownish grey body with no zigzag pattern. A metallic appearance is created when small white flecks happen to be on the back and sides.

Northern Zigzag salamanders prefer damp habitats on forested slopes, rocky hillsides, cave entrances and leaf litter. Their diet is made up of small invertebrates, more specifically beetles and spiders. They are among the most abundant salamander species in Tennessee. When the months get warm during summer time, these animals retreat to underground burrows or cave entrances where it is damp and cool.

The Red backed salamander, another species of salamander looks exactly the same as a Northern zigzag salamander. Hence these two are confused very often. The lifespan, diseases and size of the home range of Northern zigzag salamanders are still not known.

Clouded salamander

Clouded Salamander, Aneides ferreus

Bill Bouton Wikimedia Commons

The Clouded salamander is small in size growing up to a length of about 5 inches.   They are usually dark brown in color with gold or brass flecks. The most distinct feature of this species would be their toes. They are quite long and ends with a squared tip. The tails help them when climbing. These salamanders inhabit older stand forests that can hold moisture on the forest floor as debris get collected. They also inhabit in certain areas where loose debris of logs are found. However, their range is quite limited. In America, these creatures are found to be living across the coast of Oregon to northern California.

Clouded salamanders feed on a wide variety of invertebrates such as ants, spiders, mites, millipedes, centipedes, sowbugs and termites. Young ones consume smaller preys but gradually take on larger preys as they grow bigger. We use lungs in order to breathe. Similarly, these type of salamanders use their skin to breath. Hence they require moist environments when living on land. One interesting thing about these creatures is that, they defend their territories. Males are aggressive when it comes to territorial clashes and would not hesitate to fight with others.

Green salamander

Green salamander <u>Brian Gratwicke</u> Wikimedia Commons

Green salamanders are small in size and could be considered the only salamander species to have green markings in North America. The distinct yellow- green appearance helps determine this species very easily. However, the younger ones possess yellow limbs and lesser patterns on their upper body. Green salamanders have large eyes and their toe tips are square in shape. Adults usually grow between 8 – 12cm in length. However, the females tend to be little bigger than the males. These creatures are very active during night time when months are warmer, heavily relying on their body patterns in order to avoid predators at day time. Green salamanders consume spiders, snails, slugs and small insects. They prefer their habitats to be damp or within shaded crevices of rocks.

Green salamanders hibernate during the end of each year, precisely from December to March. The population of these creatures are at risk due to habitat destruction and manmade developments like roads. They are most commonly sighted in South Central Ohio though isolated populations are found in Georgia as well as North and South Carolina. The green salamander is enlisted as threatened in Pennsylvania. However, it is considered to be endangered in Mississippi, Ohio, Indiana and Maryland.

Author Bio

Fathima Zahra Jazeel

Was born in Sri Lanka and completed her G.C.E Advanced Level in the Bio Science stream. She completed her BTEC Level IV Edexcel Professional Diploma in Teaching in the year 2013 and currently works as a teacher while following the BTEC Level V Edexcel Professional Diploma in Advanced Teaching leading to a professional degree. Her passion for journalism made her engage in writing for both local as well as international newsmagazines.

Her family had been rearing parrots as pets for decades which motivated her to be a local voluntary social worker to create awareness about conserving animals in the wild.

Our books are available at

1. Amazon.com

2. Barnes and Noble

3. Itunes

4. Kobo

5. Smashwords

6. Google Play Books

This book is published by

JD-Biz Corp

P O Box 374

Mendon, Utah 84325

http://www.jd-biz.com/

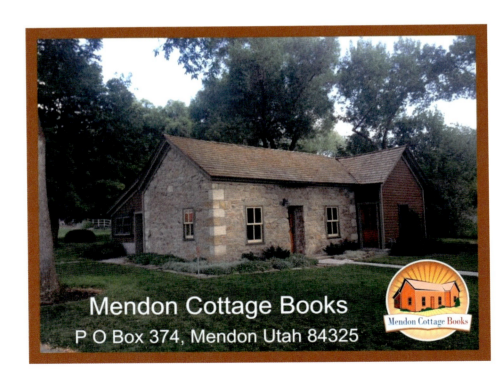

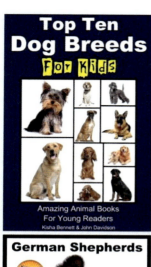

Top Ten Dog Breeds For Kids

Amazing Animal Books For Young Readers

Kisha Bennett & John Davidson

Poodles

Dog Books for Kids

K. Bennett

Labrador Retrievers

Dog Books for Kids

K. Bennett

German Shepherds

Dog Books for Kids

K. Bennett

Rottweilers

Dog Books for Kids

K. Bennett

Boxers

Dog Books for Kids

K. Bennett

Golden Retrievers

Dog Books for Kids

K. Bennett

Beagles

Dog Books for Kids

K. Bennett

Yorkies

Dog Books for Kids

K. Bennett

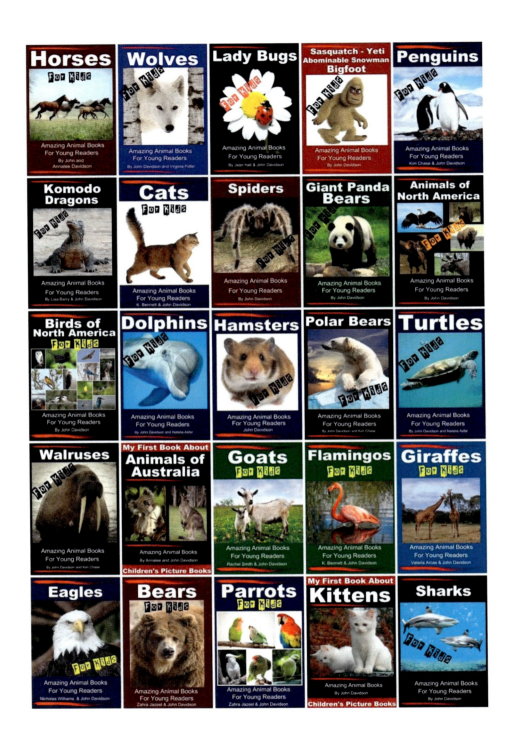

Made in the USA
Coppell, TX
16 May 2021

55780999R00026